Come, Let Us Be Joyful!

THE STORY OF HAVA NAGILA

by Fran Manushkin

ILLUSTRATED BY

Rosalind Charney Kaye

UAHC PRESS · NEW YORK

For Hannah Naomi Buzil
—FM
In memory of my father,
Dr. William Charney
—RCK

Hava Nagila

Come, let us be joyful
and let our happiness overflow.
Come, let us be joyful
and let our happiness overflow.
Rise, rise, o brethren
Rise, o brethren, with a happy heart.

It is a fine thing to be joyful. And is anything more joyful than coming home after a long journey? I'm going to tell you a story about a song and a journey home that took two thousand years!

This story begins thousands of years ago, when the Jewish people lived in the Holy Land. They planted vineyards there and fields of golden wheat, and in Jerusalem, they built a great Temple unmatched for holiness and beauty. But, sadly, as time passed, the land fell into war after war, and conquering armies destroyed much of it. Most of the Jews were driven into exile, to wander the earth.

Through these hundreds and hundreds of years, the Holy Land suffered too. The people were few and scattered, and the land barren; even the desert winds seemed to howl from loneliness.

God heard these cries, and the voices of the Jewish people, who prayed every day for a return to Jerusalem.

One hundred years ago, some men and women decided it was time to return home. Over their Sabbath suppers, they talked about it:

"Let us return to rebuild our land!" said a gray-bearded sage.

"Right now?" asked the town peddler.

"Why not now?" smiled the sage.

"We will make the desert bloom!" declared the woodsman.

"Ha!" mocked the pickle-man. "You will raise only mosquitoes!" But who listened to him? No one!

So gathering up their featherbeds, their candlesticks, and their memories, the villagers set forth on a journey. To keep their spirits up, they sang their favorite melodies.

One of these was a little tune, without a name, and totally lacking in words.

When the settlers reached the Holy Land, the milkmaid marveled, "Jerusalem is golden, but it is also dusty." As she swept out an old stone house, the little tune kept her company. The woodsman also sang the tune, as did the pickle-man and the cobbler.

Before long, the settlers began feeling at home in the Holy Land. Soon they could tell the difference between a cactus and a camel, and a donkey from a fig tree, and the Red Sea from the Dead Sea. "Ah!" declared the pickle-man. "How joyful it feels walking in the footsteps of King David!"

One day, somebody—was it the woodsman?—was walking along when he met a man who said he was a song collector.

"A song collector? What kind of job is that?" asked the cobbler.

"A fine one!" replied the man, whose name was Professor A. Z. Idelsohn. "I collect Jewish songs, and then I teach them to my classes. That way, they will never be forgotten."

Well, before you could say, "La-la-la," the woodsman and his friends crowded into the professor's small room and sang him their haunting tune.

Now, this professor had heard many fine melodies, but this one seized hold of him and refused to let go. He told his music class, "Boys, listen to this song." Well, some boys listened, and some did not.

A sandy-haired boy who did, called out, "Teacher, this tune sounds lonely. I think it wants words."

"Moshe Nathanson, you are right!" his teacher agreed. "Let us see who can write the best words."

Now, Moshe was eleven years old, and no taller than a tomato vine, but oh did he love music! All week long he whistled and hummed that tune as he trod the rocky streets of Jerusalem. Moshe's steps were quick and lively—so quick the tune had to hurry to keep up! And the faster Moshe sang it, the merrier the song became!

"I have made a wistful song happy!" Moshe marveled. "Now I am going to give it some happy Hebrew words." That night, by flickering lamplight, Moshe made them up. "Mama! Papa!" he called. "Come listen." And, for the first time, the world heard these joyful words:

HAVA NAGILA!
HAVA NAGILA!
HAVA NAGILA!
V'NISM'CHAH...

And what do these words mean? "Come, let us be joyful and let our happiness overflow!"

When Moshe finished singing, his papa beamed, "Moshe, what a song!"

And his mama said, "What a son!"

The next day, Moshe sang the song to his class. The professor declared, "Your words are perfect! From now on, 'Hava Nagila' will be our class song."

But did Moshe's words stop there? Of course not! His classmates took "Hava Nagila" home to their families, and soon it was sprouting up everywhere, like sunflowers in the newly planted Negev.

As young men and women drained swamps and swatted mosquitoes, they sang "Hava Nagila" like this:

Hava SWAT! *nagila*
Hava SWAT! *nagila*
Hava SWAT! *nagila*
V'nism'chah . . .

And as girls in Jaffa picked juicy oranges and squeezed them, they sang it like this:

Hava Squeeze! *nagila*
Hava Squeeze! *nagila*
Hava Squeeze! *nagila*
V'nism'chah . . .

Fishermen on the Red Sea crooned "Hava Nagila" to wake up the fish.

Kibbutzniks sang the song around their campfires to drown out the howling wolves!

Soon, no wedding was complete without "Hava Nagila" and a happy hora.

As time passed, more people came to settle the land.

✡n that great day in 1948 when the Holy Land became the new state of Israel, "Hava Nagila" was sung from Safed to Tel Aviv, from En Gedi to Mount Carmel

It was a perfect old-new song for a brave old-new country!

Today, people sing "Hava Nagila" all over the world. You may wonder, how did Moshe Nathanson feel about this? He was pleased, of course. But Moshe was not a person to brag, so few people know his story. That is why I am telling it to you.

Now, tell me, don't you agree: Is there anything happier than arriving home after a long journey? And singing a joyous song? Of course not.

But, I'm sure you knew that already!

About Moshe Nathanson

The story of Moshe Nathanson's life is as happy as his song "Hava Nagila"! Moshe was born in Jerusalem in either 1899 or 1900. (In those days, people didn't pay as much attention to birthdays as we do now!) It was clear from a young age that Moshe had a wonderful voice. Indeed, when he was five, Moshe was a soloist in his synagogue choir, standing on a chair so that the congregation could see as well as hear him.

By the time Moshe was eight, he was acting as cantor at synagogue services. His lyrics for "Hava Nagila" were inspired by lines from the Hebrew liturgy: *Zeh hayom asah Adonai; nagila v'nism'chah vo* ("This day the Lord has made; let us be happy and rejoice in it").

In 1922, continuing his musical education, Moshe emigrated to Canada and then to New York City, where he studied voice, graduating from the Institute of Musical Art (now called the Julliard School of Music).

For forty-six years, Moshe Nathanson was the cantor at the Society for the Advancement of Judaism, in New York City, working alongside Rabbi Mordechai M. Kaplan, the founder of the Reconstructionist movement. Moshe married a woman named Zipporah, and they had three children—a son, Yoram, and twin daughters, Deena and Nomi. Moshe's daughter Deena says that when she tells people at weddings that her father wrote "Hava Nagila," nobody believes her. Now, perhaps, they will!

Moshe Nathanson is remembered by his students, friends, and family as a man with a lively, warm, and magnetic personality. Once, when he was hit by a car and had a broken leg, Moshe composed songs from his hospital bed, playing on his mandolin.

Moshe Nathanson continued writing songs all of his life, including the musical setting for the beginning of the *Birkat HaMazon* (Grace after Meals), which is so familiar that most people believe it to be a folk melody. He also collected and introduced many Palestinian and Israeli songs on his popular radio show called "The Voice of Jerusalem." Many of his song lyrics are collected in his book, *Shireynu*, and he made one recording, "Sing Palestine."

Moshe died on February 21, 1981, after a long, fulfilling life.

Moshe Nathanson as a soldier in the Turkish Army.

Publishers Note

The story that you have just read, *Come, Let Us Be Joyful!* is the tale of how a twelve-year-old student, Moshe Nathanson, and his teacher, A. Z. Idelsohn, collaborated in turning a niggun from Sadigora into the song "Hava Nagila." While researching this book, the author found numerous references which support Moshe Nathanson's claim to writing the lyrics. Among them are *Hava Nagila: The World's Most Famous Song of Joy* (Shapolsky Publishers, 1988), by Cantor Sheldon Feinberg, *Jewish Music: Its Historical Development* by Abraham Z. Idelsohn, with a new introduction by Arbie Orenstein, (Dover Publications, 1992), and *The Concise Encyclopedia of Jewish Music,* by Macy Nulman (McGraw-Hill, 1975).

However, A. Z. Idelsohn, in his *Thesaurus of Hebrew-Oriental Melodies,* asserted that *he* created the lyrics. The *Encyclopaedia Judaica,* in its entry on Idelsohn, accepts this assertion, as does Irene Heskes in her book *Passport to Jewish Music* (Greenwood Publishing Group, 1994).

Both A. Z. Idelsohn and Moshe Nathanson had distinguished careers: Idelsohn as a musicologist and Nathanson as a cantor, teacher, and composer of many songs, including the well-loved melody for the *Birkat HaMazon.*

Who "really" wrote the lyrics for "Hava Nagila"? We do not know definitively. The song was never copyrighted, and the claims of both individuals boast supporters in the academic and music communities. The origins of the song and its composition have entered the realm of Jewish folklore.

One thing we *do* know for sure: As long as there are reasons to rejoice, people the world over will be singing "HAVA NAGILA," the world's happiest song of joy.